STAMPING GROUND

Poems by
David Rigsbee

ardis / ann arbor

Some of the poems in this collection were previously published in: *American Poetry Review, Aspen Leaves, Cold Mountain Review, Gulfstream, New South Writing, The Ohio Review, Public Fantasies,* and *The St. Andrews Review.*

STAMPING GROUND

CONTENTS

for Carolyn and Joseph

I

Even those I loved the best
Are strange—nay, rather stranger than the rest.

—John Clare

The Lower Mysteries

In the morning I sit
before the high mirror
waiting for a verdict
on the lower mysteries.

Here comes the judge.
All rise. He takes
his place behind my eyes
and sits deep in his robes.

After a time the jury
files in like cylindrical
weights pushed gently along
the balance beam of old scales.

Mr. Chairman, have you
reached a decision?
We have, Your Honor.
The defendant will rise.

We find the defendant
innocent on all counts.
The judge bangs the gavel.
A sigh goes up from the body.

Goodbye

Those heroes are at the window again.
After six months, now they're back:
the artist who boiled your soul in his oils,
the boy who shot off his foot to offer you,
the magician with his Tarot pack
and levitation tricks.

Naturally you turn to stare at them
because they preen wonderfully
and strike corny poses
reminding you of snapshots from long ago
with your moony face
included in the corner.

I would be bored with them
if they weren't so startling,
suddenly lurking in the window when I come out
of the bathroom. But they are eager to please;
their faces float across the glass
like harlequins dancing over a fairground.

I can see that you are fascinated
by these infrequent visits
and it is to you that they direct
most of their devices—
winking, crossing their eyes,
blowing their noses.

They are telling you
that they want you to join them,

that they will abduct you,
if necessary,
according to the rite,
knowing your weakness for anything gypsy.

So you rise, frowning, and leave the room.
Immediately they vanish.
The moon shines in, and the little stars.
I stand in the half light:
one leg, one arm,
an eye.

The Triangle

1.

I am standing at the center of a triangle
watching the spiraling descent of birds.

Your coat lies in the grass, twisted outwards
as if removed hurriedly, and dust is just now beginning
to settle on the road.

There is a kind of nostalgia for this road
that unravels confused journeys,
for the symmetry of eternal returns
and shoes lugging blood at the end of twilight
down the beach to the sea.

This triangle was another figure, now wrecked.
I regard these bounds with curiosity.
The primary sensation is of waste.

There is this to understand:
men starve in the middle of mandalas,
their minds twice polarized.
They are stronger than me and yet do not move.
Their corners are fastened by familiar people
holding their light like sick sparrows.

2.

You are sitting beside your beautiful mother.
She is dying. Literally disappearing into
the experience of it. No one is the wiser.

Words drop away from us like knives
but the deathly sick are not their casualties.

You place your hand
on her forehead white as a lampshade,
holding back the light that tries to escape.
This is part of it too.
Your hand holds the light back also.
That is part of it:
to push back the light that burns the body
to prove in short that there will be resistance
as you want to believe.

You speak to her and she answers with eyes
standing on the shore of her blood.

3.

I have been sitting alone all day drawing birds
like I have never seen before in nature.
Their eyes dangle sprung from their foreheads.
The rest of their features are like motley shingles
slapped carelessly across a wall.
It is very easy to reduce a face to its meaning.
I have drawn enough birds today to wallpaper a small room.
Each could be another life, but it isn't.

I wanted in some way to compensate with this,
a flock that would never fly for the ocean
but silently draw you back to me
when the bloody shoes have walked out there.

4.

Your letters arrive every day,
a faint pulse recorded on a graph.

I know that explanations
do not even shade the breaking horror,
the fissures inside and between.

I know the terms that fling a cheesecloth
over the cracks, how words break down
to "is" and "is not"
"maybe" and "no."

You are saying things are worse
and it is all breaking.
I do not have to read letters to know that.

5.

I want to record these things:

that I believe all the ignorance killing us
and this death opening

that a mandala is a silent place and I am not convinced
of its peace
that a triangle is ruled at each of its points and I
am the ruler of only one

that the birds have no eyes because they will home
anyway and in that sense they resemble our enemies

that you are reducing me to a way of understanding me
and I am doing the same to you
it gives us something to rely on when the bed
stops shaking

that I know your hand is caressing her forehead and it is
hot and filled with light

that I know she is staring at you with a radiance and it
will never work I know

that you will walk away
with her light in your hands

After Hearing a Premonition By a Friend, of My Death Next Friday

From the dead of winter I look out
and see that I am walking down the road
in a heavy snowstorm. It is as though
I am thinking with someone else's brain
of a journey that won't be mine.

The snow flies in horizontal bursts.
I have the feeling that I am watching
windows being smashed.
Honest to God I don't know
why I am here.

I look down at my coat and pants
and they are white.
I seem to become snow,
collecting what I am about to be
and walking with it back into myself.

The snow is like little pieces of glass
that rise and fly back into place
becoming windows again to stand behind
again to watch the snow fly
and a man walking through it down a road.

The Arguments of Statues

The days unhook from me and begin
a drift into a great inward lake,
riding heavy as barges on the water.
I no longer expect my mind to win
the life of my body which is constant.
Each day's possibility drops slowly
like weather from a foreign country
and with my lighter weight I rise
through the long hours to night.

Today, huddled through the window
and bending from one side to the other,
the trees seemed like a crowd of arrivals
waiting for a slow train to pull out.
I have never gone into those woods
they are so impenetrable and dark.
Yet people disappear there and reemerge
and the higher sun crams their shadows,
which were once long, back into them.

Sometimes I walk in the park and the statues
there loom from their bases in an intense
but useless way: huge presences
where dogmas chipped the stone and died
or left off broken; it doesn't matter.
I want to blow the statue out of myself
but I can find no hard evidence
along my skin, just the same skin
tracing a border along legs of stone.

Sometimes too, when I am riding like one

on a horse with two feet reared
(as though suddenly startled by a snake)
she will stop and say, No, make love to me.
And so I thought this also was stone,
but it responds with the skin, makes
a pain like a man standing among trees,
trying to unfold his shadow, trying
to feel a light that will not break him.

Night at Ryan's Pond

1.

Like sweaty steam radiating
from a horse's back, little coils
of fog rose off the pond
and silently moved across it.
Still light at nine o'clock,
the first car lights felt their way
along a dirt road a little way off,
occasionally reaching through the trees
then pulling back as though bitten.
The engines would stall, wedged in some
double-clutching, transmission's limbo.
But eventually they passed.
We saw the ripcords of dust swelling
on the sky.
                    "Do you think
he will come here?"
"No," she answered.
We began to put together a fire
with damp sticks from his pile
and our *Times* and listened to it,
the near-living hiss and spit.
"Billy Ryan gets home late,"
she said, "and besides, he's usually
drunk." She said nothing else
of this man, a wildman possibly,
her friend I never knew.
We sat with blankets covering us
and watched a glow spread up the cinderblocks.
The fog arrived over her arms,

planting, goosebumps. We sat closer, rumps
touching, light lambent and orange
across our faces.
She turned her body to mine,
the "poor excuse" as she once put it
to a black dude. We stared
at each other's poor excuses.
She: "Honest to God
that looks like a man to me."
To me, where I sat and why.
Because a London cutpurse
went unhung.

                    2.
Afterwards we leaned back
and divided the sweat between us.
She lit up and said,
"Do you believe in devils?" I said
I did and flicked a cigarette butt
into the one eye of the fire.
With one eye she followed
the cold trajectory.
"Luck," I said. "No, a man."

A little man began to unfold
inside me, making me feel
like a Chinese box.
I felt homunculus eyes
looking through mine to the woods,
afraid of this woman
and her ax-toting hillbillies,
afraid her desire would slip back
to the trailers, to the pale babies
and the drunk men lying
unbuttoned in the grass.

He turned my head to her
and she knew who I was.
The way he spoke to her
was all a cultivation. She knew
it too and he was afraid.
"I'm not sure I'm the right
person for you," she said.
He acted hurt and made a frown
which she knew from the faces
of other little men.
But it was different now
with the fire beginning to dim,
going out like it had started.
His frown too was about to go out
for the last time and she watched it
slowly vanish into the patience
of his face. Then nobody came
around the pond or snaking
through the fog. He held her
like he was somebody else.
He watched himself do it.
She backed down, saying
just that she was afraid of the way
his mind played, said sometimes
he was like a beautiful woman, and at others
they were like "spirits"
(admitting the presumption
and all the devils now
prancing from him to her). He
was flattered, not to say gratified,
and rebuilt the fire. They saw
the fog not stopping.
Nobody came and they spent
the night together alone,

locked and still because it
was cold and because it was night.

The Prophecy of the Wax Figure

1.

I wait in a cold room for a breath
of perfume. The sun stares through the window
and leaves swish at it, explaining themselves.
I have been staring at this object now
for an hour and finally I understand it.

The wax figure consists of a man running
just about to reach the edge, and behind him
of another darker figure, also running arms
outstretched as though receiving the effect
of absence that the first man gives off.

2.

I try to make out the expressions
on their faces, but they are very small
and rough. In any event, the light is waning.
That is why the first man is almost to the edge.

3.

That is also why the second figure runs
holding arms out at full length,
not to catch the first man's escape
that lives for an instant in his slipstream:
the second figure is after that man himself.

4.

The falling light puts their edges in relief.
Now in the twilight, it is easier to recognize
that they are engraved in our likeness.

5.

At the moment of complete darkness
I touch the first figure and mash him out.
Then I knead the wax around
until I can feel that the second figure's
arms are stretched around
and that its hands implore its rounded back.

6.

I leave the room where you have not returned.
I leave the ball of wax for you, a clump
to melt down and raise the dead.

The Country of My Love

The rug burns in a labyrinth of colors.
It is at a delicate moment in its creation.
The Arab waits for the young man who
promised the delivery of thread. He wipes
sweat away with the mop of his sleeve.
His wife is dead, and sons he did not have
do not come dangling home on the end
of a rope tied to a sacred cow's nose.
He turns the hung rug to face Damascus
because the sun is now in the west.
The road there is not filled with pilgrims.

These chairs are the least of my threats,
whittled from the mother-tree, but no less
tools of another's falling. A man fell
from the lowest branch and did not hit
but bobbed a little, crooking his vision
at the joint, and stared at the English
countryside with eyes like subway tokens.
He also had an erection and would have been
embarrassed except that it was late.
That is why I will not mind standing
for good when these chairs are removed.

At this table there was once a dinner
set for three priests. I was not there.
I bought it for two hundred and seventy-
five dollars and got a certificate.
The first time I tried to move it into my
house a foot came off and a claw gouged

a wound in the rug. I put it back together
with glue, but I never trusted it again
and sat holding down the claws with the soles
of my shoes whenever I ate. No one noticed,
not even the maid when she would stoop.

They say that in a mirror everything
is reversed. I believe it. On my wall
there is a great framed mirror such as
wicked queens were said to interrogate.
I look into the mirror and see three priests
wiping lamb-grease from their lips and smiling
at a young man and a shy woman who is serving.
I see a young boy dollop from a tree branch,
get up and run over to a great herd of cows
marshalled by a family of rich Persians
in the oriental rug business. I do not

see a moving van framed in the window,
three men unloading their hand-trucks
and checking their watches. I do not see
a history of Wedgwood, Gorham and Baccarat
packed to the ceiling in excelsior and
Styrofoam. I do not see a tear-streaked
queen in a pant-suit saying leave
the bed for the bastard. Until a man
pardoned himself, removed the mirror
and left the nail in the wall to stick,
I knew this was the country of my love.

The Tortoises Go Home Tonight

We lie down together, so horizontal
no wonder the sky peels back in an arc
and something pivots through the underground.

The tortoises go home tonight
through clouds sudden as a scream
to spill a bellyache of eggs
down nocturnal craters. Their heads
retract, after emptiness.

Light goes from the room
but you fidget and test the darkness
with the edge of your hand. It is so quiet
my heart climbs out of its skin to rest
in the space between us.

You want to curl your hand
around creatures like these
but they never give you the chance.
Even by the dark they see
the brain at work in back of your eyes.

The Signatures

I trace the walls of my room
to find out how actuality
is enhanced by traps.

But always I stop
to consider the documents
on the big oaken desk.
There is a dotted line
at the bottom of each of these
and each is an addition to the last.
Of course they are forced confessions.
No one is fooled by that, least of all me.

Nevertheless I stamp my face on every page
until it becomes my face:
poor image I'm afraid,
but that's the price of distance
when I pull away
and a consequence that never concerns me.

Only now the abandonment
of a mouth I never meant to give
of eyes looking always in
and of skin that blows off like erasures
astonishes.

I have never seen this man before in my life.

Her Afterlife

The worst of it was that everything was taken away
except desire, and that was her shadow's spine
where nothing clung, gray and terrified
like a bat, and in that seeming body she appeared
as on the last day when the city was swarming
with escape artists, the day she went up in smoke
and dropped that smoke's shadow like a snake
straight into Hell beneath its fire of shame
that kept her burning and a woman forever.

There she could draw up a separate peace
with her old cast-off, reinvent the boring life
she wouldn't have when flesh was the amusement
that wrapped her spirit around until she met
that beautiful effeminate stranger who turned up
full of graces and fantasies one day in her city.
Then she could understand nothing but led him away
continually with extravagant gifts and finally the sty
of her sex until he would otherwise starve.

Behind her back they began to turn against her,
those other men, said she was a whore and a sow
who would smother their future in her excrement.
One day he changed too, came mumbling some crap
about duty and gods. No remorse showed on his face
but stayed pinned behind his teeth when he told her
he was leaving. He only stared down, pulled
the leaves from a clover and said it was not his choice.
When he sailed he could not recognize her wail of smoke.

Now, when she saw his approach, led by the hand

of that tall, hollow-eyed creature of the inhuman
voice, she desired again to throw herself on him,
to beg him to remember his love for her.
But she saw the tears sheet his eyes over
and far fields open with warriors left and right.
So when he opened his mouth and held out his hand
which was filled with the gross weight of that living,
she was repelled and turned away, his enemy forever.

Engaged Music

If you sit long enough in urine
your skin will break down.
So don't do it.

My teeth are rotting in my mouth.
I am rotting in this house
in this town in this poem.

Still, the aphids walk along
the window on their way
to the roses.
No blame.

Inside my wife there is a motor.
I oil it with apologies
for my bad life. You're not the person
I married, she says.
I'm sorry, I say

listening to the sirens
before I go off to sleep.
I would rather hear them
than anything, than Beethoven

who says at least
act
and I am not sorry

when I break.

Sitting on a Hill

The cows start, a herd
of ax-handles walking on end,
turned back to the mangers,
toting the lean white factories
the swollen milkbags
and their four helpless fingers.

A tractor crawls back from the field
like a steel-footed snail
dragging the darkness open behind it.
The dust, also, rears into bloom
or the short ghost of a bloom
awakened from under the tired wheel

as when the spirits lift
and walk behind a man,
their thighs a memory
of brightness and living, so faint
they must melt back at once,
and only the quick can see them.

So today the light falls,
steel down a canyon. Something
must fly like splinters
when the man is done with his plowing
and his animals lie down heavy-legged,
and the animals in him.

The Undivided Minds

Glen's Falls, New York

In the exquisite Federalist gardens
of the undelighted dead, in the dead of July
I undid my tie and buffed the dust
from my shoes, waiting to get the ritual
underway. The others were late; we imagined
a black Lincoln heaving at a dry pump
or the traveling grief swinging lost
somewhere in Vermont. With me, my wife
and a glib member of the clergy
stared wordless down the tarred lanes
shrewdly segregating Republicans from Catholics,
further sorted into wrought-iron enclaves:
family trees crashed into graphic charts,
the least spaces bunched near the walkway
the size of Hormel hams, commemorated
by illegibly rough and ancient headstones.
The wind had taken its rubbings from these
little angels and hung them somewhere.
As it happened, we decided to split up
and look around. It was quite hot
and our divine's forehead was shiny
with perspiration. I watched my wife
as she receded in shimmers of heat
and took no notice left or right of the stones
curious by the thousands at her feet.
I left the canon sweating, moping plaintively
around his Pontiac and walked slowly
so as to take advantage of the elm shade.

It was out of earshot from the buzz
of hot tires on the highway that I felt
alone for the first time in recent memory,
and so, I think, must she have, abstractly,
in the dust at the far end of that place.
It was not, you see, that she and I
had found separate corners to confront.
We did not grieve, not in the usual sense,
not because the air had closed in over the matron's
place, her form in rich empty cushions
that the cat sniffed. It was different
because the last focus of our undivided
minds was being lowered like a semaphore.
The earth itself soaked our contract up
no different from the oiled gravel roads
spilling away under the midsummer sun
where the branches yawed and the grass ticked.
It was a quiet touchdown, systems regrouped
around a frugal heart, unpassable pass, which
would not have helped us, if it had know how.
I stopped and looked out across the field
into the stone faces of Furies, symbolizing
these ironic reunions, and beyond to a gray tent
pitched like a dropped handkerchief under which
a man was stretching, waving his arms.

II

The Inheritance Tax

As I grew he learned to speak less
in the corona where my eyes hatched.
I knew next year could not bear
up his love and lying both: no
salve in time for a cloven foot.

Age shrank him and he trudged
across a melting heap of satisfactions,
gathered and rubbed them into his skin.
But they dripped from him where he went
like money from a nouveau riche.

I grew wild around the corner of his life.
an uprooted jungle, and calipers like pliers
raised me sweating from the ground.
In truth I only had his words to know him by:
a promise or two that limped and died

between my ear and the door slammed shut.
How much must he have recognized
when the eyes of the myth grew white
and his confessions crowded to my mouth
pretending now to have to speak.

Birds

I

He feels wings fan the light
across his lids.
He wakes and jams his little bird
of a fist to his mouth
as though to eat it, but he can't.
It is tied to his pain.
His mother pulls the hand away
because she is awake and also sees this
across slatted regions of light.
She whispers,
"No, darling, or he will fly away."

II

A hummingbird floats in a tiny fury,
indistinct except for the needle-beak,
blue head, and eyes
staring at two sides of chaos.
Small boys sneak up behind
and remove it from the air
with potholders.
They stuff it quickly into a jar
because they are squeamish
and leave for a few hours.
When they return they are
offended to find it dead.

III

My father's scalp is where they light,
the big ones preceded by claws,

by their shadows, and the shadows
of their claws.
He keeps on walking, a brave man.
They cannot lift him.
My mother turns her eyes on this
with the fascination of an owl
with holes driven straight to the eye bottoms
sunk by divination
through the breast, the gut
and feet, leaving wells
in place of tracks,
shot crows in place of pulleys.

IV

Today my plane whines
through the stratosphere
over tufted clouds drawn
stiff like the wings of herons.
The plane's wings are speared
into the fuselage.
The cross moves cautiously through the sky.
Sitting back from the window
and closing my eyes,
I dream we are standing defenseless
on opposite banks of a river.
Even the sparrows fly across
to no purpose.

V

The baby cannot sleep.
Shadows from the ceiling
glide across his eyes.
He rocks from side to side, watching,
and puts a fist to his mouth
trying to eat it like a bird.

She wakes again and whispers,
"Darling, no, or he will fly away."

VI
They leave the skull at last
and spiral out of sight.
He raises his face like a tilted cliff
when the clouds roll, opening and
closing, in from the sea,
in time to see the last black wings
push the air down and a body carried away,
its motion corkscrewing the wind over his head.

VII
The curtain flutters,
folded cloak where the sky
passes through, palm out
to receive who would not fly.

Squirrel Stew

My grandfather and his men
used to snap off the feet with knifeblades
then shuck the furred skins
and drop them into a bloody bucket.
They were dead alright but
terrorized me and I ran away
and came back to look some more.
They were a little ashamed of me, I think,
sniveling after squirrel corpses.

It didn't bother me though
when Granny Weaver died.
She was so old and next to
nothing anyway through all her fat.
She pissed all the time and they
had to bathe her.
I used to watch them
and they let me stand there
like I was nobody.
She was very pale and soft as cobwebs
and they pulled up her breasts
like dishrags and scrubbed with a sponge
but they couldn't make her any whiter
than she was.

Then the old lady left,
just wasn't there anymore,
left without a dent in the cushion.
Look, there's more to the story
than that.

My real grandmother was the next
to be old, but she couldn't be
because she wasn't.

Meanwhile we waited and ate
squirrels stewed, with gravy,
their little bones knocking on the plate.
Even now when I think about it
I get sick to my stomach.

The Wave in the Field

As I crawled under the house with my flashlight
I found the green frogs waiting for me and posing
at the finger of light that lit them one by one.
A storm was coming through the eastern sky
to short itself out here, and we huddled in the dirt
with our eyes sticking out the sides of our heads.

A late summer, late evening stillness was settling
the heat like lint across the clammy underyard
and the sound of feet clumped and wandered off
over our heads. This was a house to be buried in:
rambling, unpainted, and clapping with each clap
like a box the cemetery had thrown back.

But tomorrow, led by the wooden necessary hand
and packing their years in a lump
they were leaving for a tiny house on the edge of town
that promised nothing but to make its charity
open in proportion to its simpleness: a made-up
virtue for a house not even a specter of this one.

Neighbors came and odd relatives lugging their bloodlines.
They sat on the porch where the boards still held
with babies squirming like victims on the end of a stick.
The older kids devolved to monkies and climbed
the frail chinaberry limbs after the roosting guineas
who had refused eviction, on principle, forevermore.

The men talked of the countryside and hunting.
Someone went out to his car and brought back
the "smithereen" of a jet plane that had crashed

47

years ago near his field. They all examined this.
Old farmers were resurrected and laid to rest
again, their family trees sniffed at the stumps.

My mother sat by her father's leg, on a step-below.
He talked to her excitedly. I could not catch
much of what he said—he must have spoken with his hands.
After a while the crowd began to leave, stashing babies
and cakeplates, loitering for the usual salutes.
And the dust stood on its feet and flew away.

She had called after me for a quick goodbye
but I sat it out instead underneath the porch
and afterwards hearing his words falling so softly
that my imagination had trouble grasping them
as though the sharp edge of his life had collapsed
and cut loose the child, my twin, from his throat.

Now his speech was almost silence
like a drizzle that gathers armfuls of dust
in a gray labor and returns to earth with it.
The six feet between us was joined by the sixty
years and I felt like the little frogs
waiting to come out after the rain.

I dreamed of the house many times after that,
and I stood on its steps looking out.
But instead of the unbounded miles of cotton
there was a wave breaking across the field
with an ocean suddenly behind it, and always that water
crashed once and withdrew like a servant from the room.

Then the house and the country around it fell quiet
and waited under a bright calm endlessly.

When I Last Saw Him

When I hugged him he seemed so small
he was like a midget running out of body
and growing smaller by the minute. His story
took the evening to tell, and once in a while

he seemed to confuse me with the other one
and addressed me as her, so far had his mind
wandered. Yet had she been present she would
have heard again the things which disgusted her.

"I sat up the last nights and stared at you
sleeping, knowing I would never see you again,
and once I went into the other room and sat
watching the furniture in the dark, and imagined

my life. The next days were tame dogs
leaping upright against each other.
The baby talked, suddenly, with his fists,
damning my thighs because you had left."

Then catching himself, he paused and continued,
"It was March, when the last sleet
had popped the roads: then it was over.
But I saw her just the other day, and we talked.

Her presence made little impression on me
as though I had been warped back before it all,
except that after lunch she disappeared into the crowd,
another of a hundred stiff fur coats.

Now all over town I find the slivers buried
like straws blown wild in a tornado
and I see my body too, lodged between
each one of the ten thousand things."

III

Devil

We were going to see it all, but we
were losing sight of the dog as her
sprightly bag of old bitch-meat
sprang around the other side of the hill

where a horse named Devil was grazing
and stamping around, his tail spilled
swishing past his nuts, fanning the flies
into an aura visible around him which he

twisted from and blasted with his nose.
We walked on a path below the fence
blooming with barbs that kept us
from the hilltop and the animal.

"This is the place he first touched
my cunt." Speaking of her first one,
dead under shades and falling away.
"I was afraid, but I liked it."

The dog appeared, loping inside the fence.
The horse began to swing his head around
as though it were joined to a turret,
and he stared the dog to her haunches.

Well, he had a big number, he did.
At least innocent eyes swelled it up
for the appetite and the melodramatic
give-away, it being that time of year.

53

We kept walking. She talked of others
and motioned out spots from this history
like a guide pointing to graves on a battlefield
or the martyrs in cathedral windows.

He was there above us in his principality
of old cow-flop, lord of his cage.
The black genii of old seductions
was basking his muscles. His imitators existed:

a menagerie of quasi-inspired machos
reduced to ghosts, squatted in her brain
where she rifled through them
like oily rags on a closet floor.

So she was the first to know what
that horse was doing as he stood frozen
and forced Bess into instant subjection,
slipping tail over her ancient privates.

"It's like you just stand there and say,
'this is what you're going to get.' "
There was his silhouette and a single
part apart from the rest.

"You could do it, if you just could
open yourself enough." She mentioned
something about Catherine the Great
whose horse mashed the mare out of her,

to the horror of her clumsy menservants.
All she wanted was the nail-head lowered
gently to her, but what gentleness!
She died not yet fundamental.

Yet it occured to me that evolution
was right, where I was,
and that a horse's flower
was no thing of quality to the ladies.

"But imagine the way he drives it,"
she said, bending into the wire.
"That's nature," indicating with her arm.
I did not know that; neither did the ghosts.

How well the dog saw through the authority
or understood only as fear, I can't tell,
but she turned tail and ran, just as
quickly resuming her blithe old life.

We went down the hill to her house
and we knew. Behind us the shadows
thinned in the grass, and she looked back,
against custom, through my eyes.

Boston Woman

The Charles turns slowly into the bay
as though it had just returned from the dead.
There are few trees here but leaves enough,
flushed and heavily etched like the gentle codgers
who click down the sidewalk with their canes.
Soon the leaves will click as they drop and heap
withering on itself into great brown piles.

Last night I met a man who knew nothing.
Today he could plop to the pavement
like a ripe peach and be satisfied
that something outlasts him.

But I lie here in a map of sweat
like someone at the end of a long holiday.
The city jams in and hoists me up
into a point surrounded with strangers
who desire me and say it is no coincidence.
I think of a man in a distant town.
I knew him once. Was he no different
than these, with his wife like a second
skin and his empty pockets?

Now the feel of hours and the wild
hydrant-dance of summer children
fill the city up, to this very door.
Little water drops lay for a while
on my breast, then roll off by slow
gradations to this bed, the ocean.

In the Night

Confined to my time, and to my house
by leaf-fallings and short circuits
in the System—bonds gnashed in two
by misunderstandings and enmity—
I sit like one in a doctor's office
awaiting the white-frocked messengers.
Benign, or malignant? How did
the body make out in its border wars?

Through the window the night, a dusting
of stars. Even they are oppugnant,
flying apart, memoryless. History
forges a horseshoe around my heart.
(For the night-mare, or a run of luck?)
And if my loves, now scattered out,
appear to have once exploded like a suitcase
dropped to the open road on a holiday

does this mean we too are flaming worlds
obsessed with parting and black frontiers?
The retrograde motion of the visible planets
is just an illusion owing to their distance
and the fact that we spin on the same
plane like skaters on an ice pond.
Some overtake, and some fall slowly back,
but if the ice breaks: they become as stars.

Sitting here, shuffling a deck of cards
aimlessly, I am of two minds. There will
be no messengers showing up to announce

what I need or need not hear: either
no sanctuaries exist for the backwards;
or this night's omens tacitly approve
these detonations, this life paid out in ruptures,
this momentary lethargy, and the artless heart.

The Scene of the Accident

She was the next to get up from the wreck
and stared a frost into me
as I stood on the other side.
It was night. I couldn't see very well.
The bent headlights stabbed the smoke,
crisscrossing out beyond my vision.
So I remember how improbable it was
that I should remember her look at all
but that it was generated
beyond the startled heap and stuck horn.
As though someone had died inside
who had not, with no thoughts
toilers behind a mask, and that torn away,
she crossed over to me
flashing her two continuous
shocks of light and I knew
that she was receding the closer
she came and would have stepped
straight into me had she not stopped
suddenly and turned around without a word
to be now bending over the door
gone back, the window mapped and falling in,
to look through it nearer, intensely,
wiping the frost away with her sleeve.

Summer Dreams

Talcottville, New York

That day the cycles hammered through town
riding the punks on their way to twilight.
"It's strange how I split myself," she said,
"into two, and one goes off looking for the
impossible and the other follows to murder it."

Two swallows screaked on a telephone wire.
Two flights of stairs lumbered to the balcony
and a dust-gray nest encrusted in the eave.
We sat under it all on the stones in the water-
blue evening feeling the shadows die into one

great shadow and the ground suck back its dust.
"I can't get out from under my dreams
lately. They are too real and they hurt me.
The man who left me, I left too. It was
just impossible. You know. Now he comes back,

and I don't know where my mind is living,
here—or there." She smiled at me and that
was her question: love or simply self-denial.
On the road the cyclists gunned back and forth,
competing because they had no one to sleep with.

We had been trying for so long to push over
the good and evil, the waking and the dreams,
and we found ourselves each morning in the same
room, terminating every night in the same bed
on which we rolled over into the same dreams.

Now, just because it was being said like pushed-over stones in a little dump of a town on the cusp of summer, there was no past that wouldn't sink with the weight of her heaviness, there was no man who wouldn't die because of a dreamless sleep.

IV

The Sum of It

We heard of some who were banished, a purge's
dust, where muttling pigeons had no capital
to haunt, no time to fold under wings.

We had been waiting months for the river to move,
watching ice grow down the cedar trunks on the bank
like fists about to strike a door.

We kept bread in cellophane to protect it
as by some transmutation it would finish
into muscle, maybe something more, who knows.

We knew there was no carping at ghosts,
their turned-away gestures shrieked indifferently,
all the souls made light by an old heaviness

all the souls traveling like index fingers
pointed up to God, traveling as breath
rushes headlong on a razorback of frost.

We stood on the bank, our breath evanescent
over the river like the pouring of a dead star,
a blind train strung freezing across the night.

Somewhere they looked for it, now almost
transparent, the dead hare between our feet,
the aborted blind babies there, curled treacherously.

No Time

Suddenly he reared up and struck his chest
as we drove back from Rochester in my car,
and panic struck me too, to see a man die.

He didn't; he eased down and sat a moment
squeezing the rhythm *by will* back into his
cavity and watched the flatland slipping by.

All the time it happens, he explained, sighing
with such peace that the invisible clocks
melted away in shame. He was not shamed by his

leaping pump, but the fringes were drying up
already and rattled in the eaves. His lips drained
dead for instance in those few minutes afterwards;

an old erosion too had washed thatch from his head.
The secret police had condemned that property
and spat on a hidden box of gold. Such was fate.

Yet I knew he was secretly afraid that he
might not get back the time, the time living
in that long march of songs: a paradox.

He was quiet for many miles to come, only
to say the houses are dark, but the people
darker, the houses would say, if they could.

The Long Winter

Times we thought that we would be busted:
an abrupt, massive doorknock like a dead tree
crashing in a winter forest of shivering souls

and the rheumy Man entering, reciting
our flown rights in a deadpan civics voice
while his marionettes webbed our secrets up.

It was a metamorphosis out of season
that forced our closet frights to take skins
and enter, no-knock, the corners of our eyes.

It was not natural to have lived as we did.
The breath of Baptists would seep up when
the clothes sifted to the floor and voices

shot up from memory like leaping dogs with Jehovah's
name hanging on their teeth, but I refused the
image for the thing: the accusatory glue unstuck.

We had left our strangers to spend the winter
in a two-part choir, singing our only sin over
the splintered Commandment that skewered all the rest.

Refused to mewl in that season's fist.
The snow danced everywhere: pork barrel
ethics froze us to dreams of liberation.

Dog Days

Cats and dogs are wearing the faces of people
I know. In the dim light one's heart hums
like a dradle, and August drips to its knees.

The porchlight is a beacon for hairy moths. The air
is thick with them, but the spiders are bored.
Swayback mares stand on the hill like bent oil drums,

their lids painted with flies, spouts pried
apart by ephemeral creatures. I heard plates
crashing in the kitchen, nearby a carving

of Christian kitsch. My friends bristle
and look to the side of me to see if I
am there. I am under a bush, asleep after losing

a fight and the nails of two fingers. There is
a spattering of starlight through the leaves
as though the tired painter flicked his brush

in disgust, knowing the house was not worth it,
the wife drumming her nails; meanwhile crickets
sing like a jack unpinned under a heavy car.

How many Augusts left to crush a hobbled faith?
The animals are far away, asleep; food lying
in the dish and what's between us we can't eat.

Dumping the Ghosts

Cupids come off the slabs lacking expressions.
This is the story of memory in its habitat: bones
on a stretcher, fey ceremonies in the little ditches.

What god would surround himself with eunuchs?
Faces on the stones do not remember
All the town with mortar in its veins, and some

insane went on the record. My boss was a stone
I picked up in a ditch, but everyone thought
he was the implacable gauze who signed

my parole each month with a shudder and left
for his stint on the ramparts. True,
I was the son of ghosts and came by my flesh

underhandedly, but no one coveted the frail,
bastard treasure like me, ancestorless, until
the weary circles brought me back to nothing.

The sad cortex slaked its dust, mainlining.
Lives went to death and living death
at the actual short ends of unreal fiats.

Then a lover came and a death angel too.
I could not tell the difference between them.
They were offering the same gift.

Lunchtime

Daylight on the trough: a gathering of vet-
eran and neophyte Its. In addition to pigs,
peacocks. In addition to peacocks, humble

integers in a magic ring. Enter and they
disperse, staring at mute heaven, leaving
the slops. But from a distance they shine

and assume shapes like an amorphous organism
or a marching band at halftime, or cloud
patterns over Cuba seen from a satellite.

What's it to a man if his passion and success
smash each other out in a puff of dust?
We could see from the window the grim lips

that seemed to gnaw the faces they grew on.
One lip was desire, Vallejo said, but the other
was jealousy, and their kiss was the suck of death.

No one kissed these. We watched the cold men
pass by the hedges, fast or slow as the situation
dictated, but always with care and a secret

knowledge that the molecules of the ground might
prove feeble enough to take them in like a trap-
door woman, the one who turns men to beasts.

Sleepwatch

Tiny lives suspended in the ice become trash
and flow away. Meanwhile we only stand; time
passes us, and we stare at the white until it thaws.

Then we ride through the gaps like crazy blind men.
Only sleeping becomes our sanity when we're
tired of the damned day and metabolic tides peel back

through the eyes and quench our brains. Then someone
is there riding alongside when time has run out
and the sleeper sleeps. It is a patience that knows

nothing comes, except rarely. Then it stops and stands
like a Beefeater before mocking schoolchildren
for the sake of the other who knows the neighborhood

of death already and not always how to get back.
There are times when he sleeps too
and the blindness opens to murky icebanks, catatonic

trees, and stiff rivers, because no eyes are needed
to negotiate the way down the wide tubes of limbo.
There is still the sky we know of night, the radiant

dust of dead stars and breath puffing out
like a spinnaker sail. Then down drops the tide,
crossing over, six feet, enough to ground a man.

The Beginning

Before we sailed from Aulis we had to kill one,
and a line. We shot an arrow and killed a rabbit.
We got into trouble. She will not have any babies,

not by me. Still I loved you, my animal sister,
as you walked away into the earth, whispering goodbye
through a ton of dust. If I can keep hands

out of my pockets. If I can keep your beauty
from being my cataract and the Devil from being
my triplicate mirrored face, then there will be

a happy hard life yet and peace to bitch in,
making flesh of the mind every fold of the way
until we become our betters, against ancient denials.

The dialectic was vicious and infinite. One wished
for a last word, a schlemiel's henbane, preferably
abstract, but no words arrive with their aspirins,

no plastic surgeons leap from the oafing phrases,
just a crude mechanism like the first wheel
to roll us to another city and its juster smog.

Take this placebo creation and give me back
the terror of dropped eggs and the thin pain of night.
We will have stories to tell, starting with our hands.

Down the Lines

Now we can see the trees
have shaken their fingers loose
and point them everywhere.
Taking our cue, we begin to go
in one of those directions,
her left foot in step with my right,
along one of those lines,
holding garbage in front of our faces
like good citizens, or ants.
Suddenly the tops of the drifts
lift and blow past a streetlight
like people in gowns crowding
to the special train. We do not
understand the form of this mob,
this old sediment like flour
that has been sifted obsessively
until only a whiteness remains
and faintly human outlines
falling, getting up, falling.
We pretend not to notice them
(it may not be a commotion after all)
but walk on with those bags
in the direction that has been shown to us.
Yet in a few hours, or decades,
they rise to their old knees,
get up and come for us.
There is no mistaking it,
how they stand in a cordon
under the dripping fir trees
and pull bodies to them.

We recognize them, our fathers
whose first images of walking
unreeled in us and in whose eyes
they stopped too. Our mothers
who stuffed their fish hearts
on floating gunpowder
in order to leap over the falls
again and die under the lilies.
Our lovers who hugged their histories
like flippers against their hearts
and went extinct. Not knowing
the protocol of this situation
we stop and put the bags
of garbage at their feet.
The bags are kicked over.
Their heads come up like radar dishes
they direct at us for minutes, or years,
without so much as a word.